The Joy of Life
Damian Jacob M. Sendler

Celebrating 18th birthday

New York, 2009

The Joy of Life
ISBN: 978-0-615-25192-9
Library of Congress Control Number: 2008908603

Copyright © 2009 by Damian Jacob M. Sendler
First Edition

Published by L.u.L.u. / Sendler Press in New York
Visit our website at www.sendlerpress.com

Summary: Book of modern poetry
[1. Literary fiction, 2. Poetry]

All rights reserved. No part of this publication can be reproduced, copied or transmitted in any form or any by means, electronic, mechanical, recording or otherwise, without the prior permission of the publishers and/or authors.

Printed in the United States of America

Dedicating my mom for her care and help

Table of contents

From the author ... page X
The breath of the wind ... page 1
We forget ... page 2
Say ... page 3
Wait ... page 4
Unashamedly ... page 5
Humility ... page 6
Morning dew ... page 7
Sky ... page 8
Spring ... page 9
Summer ... page 10
Autumn ... page 11
Winter ... page 12
Redemption ... page 13
Forgiveness ... page 14
Good wishes ... page 15
Happiness ... page 16
Casandra ... page 17
Blue ... page 18
Homeless ... page 19
Envy ... page 20
Virtue ... page 21
Passing ... page 22
Maturing ... page 23
Time ... page 24
Piktogram ... page 25
MacBeth ... page 26
Faith ... page 27

Table of contents

Dreams ... page 28
Posterity ... page 29
Bleeding heart ... page 30
Happiness and desease ... page 31
To live better ... page 32
Matthew ... page 33
Casablanca ... page 34
The time of hope will come... page 35
Traveler ... page 3
Lovers ... page 37
Mystery ... page 38
Through the forest ... page 39
I'll say ... page 40
I am thinking about you ... page 41
I thought once ... page 42
Ambitions ... page 43
He went by the park ... page 44
Forgotten, he pallored ... page 45
Children ... page 46
All night passion ... page 47
Walking with her ... page 48
I want to breathe ... page 49
I saw once ... page 50
I dreamed once ... page 51
New York ... page 52
Appropriately ... page 53
I don't know ... page 54
Many ways ... page 55

Table of contents

The splendour of love ... page 56
Effaced track ... page 57
It happened, yes ... page 58
If you only want ... page 59
Your smell ... page 60
Fight ... page 61
Everything that ... page 62
4th of July ... page 63
Through the streets of the city ... page 64
My blue dreams ... page 65
Lap of luxury ... page 66
Letters ... page 67
Colors ... page 68
Let's dance ... page 69
Undiscovered time ... page 70
In my own chair ... page 71
In my bed ... page 72
Sailing through the world ... page 73
I saw the world ... page 74
The time of my career ... page 75

from the author

It's my great pleasure to publish my first book but also be the first ever published author in my family's history. My philosophy is strictly concerned with the fact that I want to interact with people and want to exchange my ideas with others. Recently, I decided that I want to introduce a major change in my life.

I decided that as a grown person, ready to set up own goals for life I'm able not only to begin college education, but also transfer my thoughts and feelings to the greater world. I have been wondering for a long time how I can achieve that. Finally, it came to my mind that through poetry (which I enjoy a lot) I can send small messages to the world. As a young writer I tried as much as possible to persuade many things to my readers which they might not have seen in their lives until now - those are joy, anger, fulfillness, achievement, rewarding personal life, and the ability to set goals and aim toward them. As a young man I am on my pathway to make my dreams come true, and therefore, I want my readers to share the same feelings with me. I am full of joy that you are going to explore the pages of this book. Think about one, that every person has its pathway to follow and it is a good idea to know how to do that. I titled my book The Joy of Life " Celebrating 18th birthday " because I believe that this book is the highest achievement in my life regardless of any academic or personal accomplishments.

    Best wishes,
    Damian Jacob M. Sendler, Author

Let's begin the journey...

The breath of the wind

The breath of the wind moves leaves
pushes them impetuously to the front
at the same time kidnapping the tuft of lying leaves
Running spends the sound in south direction,
pushes deplorably, obsessing forestry roads.
Undetected by the people dominates sight
and delivers us the sign on the fleeting charm.
Is he the symbol of old age or maybe the symbol of the
lapse – how everyday life will run in spite of every
barriers always without the conviction.
Them more we think about this,
all the more we wander and we stand up in the
renewed astride between one and the second.
Thoughts fly with time like leaves they fly by through
the forest. You can try to chase them
but you are not ever able to overtake them.
From year to year all passes and the next pile of leaves
flies by through the period.
Before you are looked at - youth passes
 and more you are thinking about it
 the succeeding portion of the leaves passes.
Moral is such that time like the leaves passes – before
you look behind you the succeeding portion flies.

We forget

So easily to forget from where we descend
from where are our grandfathers and great grandfathers
how easily we lose our values
in this world of still unknown values.
By discovering the new country we forget about older,
and there is a feeling tied up to this land,
 which still we do not know.
But always we think and we return to the past.
The signs of suffering and bitterness are already
known to us
but what else is still waiting for us...
 can it be even worst?
We forget...
But wounds often return
and they remind without the occasion,
that obscurity is this temporary state
And once - we always return...
And we can be defended, induced for the obscurity
And in the end we reach the conviction,
that we do not know the world
And again we begin our lapses of memory.
We try without the conviction and in spite of all we
return.

Say

Say, how life will surprise us yet ;
Say, is it all worth it to strive
Say, if the face is not tired – of joy and sadness
 experienced everyday.
And so we're still able to speak,
question after question is chasing our daily life
There are more questions than corresponding people -
what's the meaning? -
in the question or in the response?
And again, my question is coming -
say, do you see the sence of this land,
or when you wake up,
do you see the sence of your existence,
whether your joy is the joy of your children ?
And in the end, is the speech a blessing or
silence leads to the success of your own soul?
Question after question comes unstopped,
but say whether you draw immeasurable satisfaction
from the fact that there is so many questions
but corresponding people only a small handful
Say, if your life has a sense of what you planned
whether it has values that you always were taught
Say, whether you are happy, whether acceptace,
which you have does not pay to much
in terms of your private life?
Tell me – are you happy?

Wait

You are the source of waiting and I have to wait
Unliberated in the embrace of love
I always look forward for your sensitivity
Forgotten or disparaged?
I'm still waiting for the touch of your love
As usually you're approaching - cold
and with the lack of feelings
 you're touching me tenderly
like a hungry dog left in kennel
for the abrasion to tears after disappearing
without shame your're sliding to me
and you're waiting until I'll forget.
I'll forget for you, but in the depths of the soul
I'll remember everything
Cold nights, not covered
with the eiderdown formed by your arms-
where were You when I was waiting for them?
Where were you gadding around
when I was waiting for You here – lonely?
Now you're talking with me-
no, I should say you're trying.
It's ain't that easy when you're deceiving me again
Maybe I look silly to you-
but indeed I'm not that stupid even though I'm with
you. I know and feel the same way as when you leave
me. But I'm still in lethargy. I'm waiting unwittingly
and I know that you'll come one day. Is it worth to
suffer that much – I don't know. But I know one – I
have been waiting and will wait always...

Unashamedly

Unashamedly is when
 you raise with the view of hatred and robbery
Unashamedly is when
you want to capture it all not thinking about others
who live in the happiness
Unashamedly is when
we think that we can do everything
Unashamedly is when
we think that God is not worth out respect
Unashamedly is when
we put our own ego over the loved ones
when we forget thanks to who we have it
When the subconscious take over the top knowing
and when we don't know when to stop
when others are asking us for it.
Unashamedly is when
 the desire of winning hurts others
and even more so if we can kill
to reward ourselves
Thoughts about own suicide are also unashamed
because who has the right
to decide about themselves
so that life and death are suited to the expiry date
Unashamedly is to pretend to live a life
of someone who we are not.

Humility

Humility is a difficult art
extremely important but still inconceivable
No matter how much in life we move
we'll never understand
that with gentleness and courtesy
we can achieve success
Being humble is to say
that above all we should respect our one's neighbour
that personal prejudices are not important
because humility is an art
rather than a question of good decorum
Humility can not be learned
but it must be purchased
Glory to those who pass through life
in sadness and joy with humble
not harming anybody.
Humble are those who always
and regardless of everything respect others
Some may say that humility
is their home life,
which protects them from evil
and keeps firmly in the right.
And you are right
humilty can elevate if time permits
but can also preserve when the situation requires it.

Morning dew

A new day is born
I look, and I see green meadows
They are reflecting with millions of colors
and a cloak of morning meadow covers them
each leaf is individually coated
and in the scale of the whole tree it recalls an icicle
Minor animals are sliding over the branches
ants are sliding on leaves
Morning dew coats grass
and when the wind blows,
the smell looms in the sky.
Millions particles of water create this theme
and when the sun is rising
everything looms as a steam.
In the zenith of sky it all distracts
and awaits the next morning
I know that when the next day I'll wake up
I'll see the water binding.

Sky

The unforgettable blue spreads over us
whenever you look up
you see the sky - blue overcoat
with a chain created of small clouds.
The sky is not only a range of clouds
it's an indicator of direction when we're confused
it's a place of each dreamer's dream
it's a place of salvation and redemption
a place where all concerns are visible
a place where life is a moderate and predictable.

Spring

Spring means rebirth
wakes up every year as a dream
brings to our hearts so much fun
booms pogrom in the hearts.
All of nature in spring blooms.
Green color coats forests
and the hope coats human hearts.
When it's late we feel bitterness
When it's premature - brings the sweetness
It's most beautiful because it's most joyful.
Nature inspires to life
and announces the advent of the new reality.
Green ivy surrounds the nature
creates a refuge not for one bird.

Summer

Summer is the period which comes after the spring
it beams his brilliance,
covers us with heat
It's a period of crazes, new adventures
Our concerns are invalid and
the heart beats harder
 because it's heated by the sun
Wind snatches our hair
and the water is beamed
by the glory of heaven.

Autumn

Autumn is a period of reflection
declining leaves create a period of reflection
we think about many matters
not yet knowing that winter is more unknown to us
In this meditation we still remain
we think and we think
and we can not get anything
Coat of colored leaves creates
and many thoughts are still forming
Summer passes and the darkness comes.

Winter

As a white mantle coats gold fields
comes after the autumn – feracious winter
A freezing ivy coats trees around
the animals are falling asleep, and they lay around
A specificity of it is still unknown to us
Bigger coldness visits us day by day
and we wonder – can it be even colder?
Everything is white in some kind of milk
Milky region creates around.
In furnaces warm fire lights
fireplaces are working
and smoke from chimneys mines
Sometimes depression comes to us suddenly
and we believe that spring is coming soon.
Sanaa are sliding over white fields
Santa Claus is coming
once again - year after year
children enjoy it and play
layer of white down is growing
and the number of responsibilities is growing.

Redemption

Redemption comes after violence
Throughout our life the power of such acts
can be so overwhelming
that when we take a backward glance
list of all sins is insurmountable.
Enumeration begins with an unintended death
What could be worse - hell or holy water?
But when our sins are not so terrible
and even slight goodness remains in us
and respect for our brothers
we may experience redemption
at the finish of our life
Are we going to be happy
and by the end of this convinced?
Unfortunately, there's no time for us now
to discuss it, because
once we'll appear before God
he'll decide what to do with us.
And once he will decide
that our sins are not so terrible
it is possible that after the bitterness of our life
we will finally experience redemption.

Forgiveness

What more difficult can meet us in life
than the injured person's forgiveness.
Bitterness of hatred and sorrow
often visit our conscience.
The more we think about this
more we worry
and we often don't know
that fault lays within us
and we cannon recognize our sin as well.
But whe conscience is finally calling
and when we have a stinging feeling in the chest
and when conscience tells us
that we'd done something wrong
we shall always appologize
and save humility before someone.
The most important is forgiveness
because personal incentives are not important
when others weep
because of us.

Good wishes

When we want
there is nothing more than our willingness
Because when we want
our will takes lead over the others
When we want
our dreams are becoming a whole
When we want
love is blowing in our house eloquently
When we want
the light in the tunnel appears
When we want
friends will love us after years
When we want
others excitement will be our joy of life
When we want
respect of your neighbour appears
When we want
the nature becomes our home
When we want – out faces can beam
When we want
Everything is possible and there are no borders for us ...

Happiness

Happiness appears when your neighbour repects you
when there is a love and you can feel it
The happiness is when your own children
love you above all they have
and when the wife is waiting for us on the morning
When we have family on our side
and good career and dreams are fulfilled.
When we can dream at any time of our life
and when we can achieve much
and during a period of sorrow
Happiness is a state of daily routine
comes to us as annual birthday.
As soon as we want we are always happy
and we know that after sorrow
joy always comes
and so in circles around the world is pending.
Happiness is a state of satisfaction
and often comes to us,
and when you want only
it stays in our hearts longer.

Casandra

There's a small lady that suddenly appears
and afterwards disappears
has so many advantages and disadvantages,
that nobody is able to enumerate them
She lives in her small apartment
overlooking the park, where
a flock of wild swans resides.
She looks at them with deep interest
and it still seems to her that
birds are like others.
After all, she sits on her leather chair
and composes songs for her mom.
She repeats this ritual daily
so her mother can have a shelf full of songs and
poems.
And try to guess what these lines are about,
and you'll know that about birds
and about Casandra itself
they are all about.
And yet – what Casandra wrote?
this will be always unknown
because she died later
and all the songs and poems
disappeared in unfamiliar spot
because she never knew her mother
and all the poems were sent by her to strangers.

Blue

Blue sky spreads out over the sea
volume of its golden spreads over beaches
It spreads over the bay of virgin islands
who discovers her beauty,
if it is still hidden in the waters
of undiscovered world
Sometimes the blue overwhelms everything
and sometimes a slight advantage it brings.
At different times storm spreads over our heads
and speaks about beauty full of blemish.
And so when we look to the sky
we see a reflection of its beauty.
A quiet soul appears immediately
I begin to think again about the charm of my future.
Blue spreads out over our heads
with clear clouds too
they crawl toward florid direction.

Homeless

He's walking on the street unnoticed by anyone
panhandles in front of the church
and traverses the streets
like a pile of unraked leaves
He walks through streets very uncertainly
nobody asks him about the hardships of his life
He has to deal with everything by himself
has to face so many obstacles in his pathway
and he has to fight for survival.
People around can not understand him
they do not want to talk with him
and more important – help him.
Loneliness often troubles
and hurts severely
because when you're lonely
it's even more difficult to live.
On additive – lack of own home
which hurts even more badly
than a murder left without judgement
Day by day is longer
and the possibility is that one day
he'll find his own home for longer.

Envy

Envy is a terrible lesson for humanity
because it can not only kill
but also hurt someone who's close to us
And despite everything appears sometimes
and hurts the entire class of human.
Envy is maily immmeasurable jealousy
when we don't know moderation
leads us to sin
and pushes the wrong way.
Always hurts others
and gives a bitter tears
It doesn't understand the words of support
and forgiveness.
The key is to make love and humility
prevalent within our hearts
and then you can be sure
that from envy we'll be kept far away
and in return, we'll offer others our help.

Virtue

Virtue is the power given from God
gives us courage and confidence
and when there is a need – protects us and assists.
Virtue is, above all, self-confidence,
that always surrounds us.
Virtue is the strength
but a the same time blockade
and provides us with purity and faithfulness,
which is give to us, though
it reminds that we are still young,
and that we still have time for everything.
Virtue is never embarrassing
rather rewards us with its beauty
until its loss doesn't come to us.
Being a person with virtue
also means being noble,
grave, wise, and sensitive.
We keep the beauty given to us at birth
and for that social respect is given to us.
When one day it will be lost
it will be definitely stored
as the best life experience.

Passing

Suddenly, his time has come
Passing, and it cannot be stopped
because passing comes with age
in the life of each adult man.
Sometimes it comes sooner or later
and when it appears to us it reveals,
that the longer time passes for us
and recalls the qualities of our life,
and plans made during childhood
and like bad thoughts it obsesses us
and still shows to us
that there is still a lot to be done,
but remember about passing.
Passing also shows
that the new generation takes top
and we shall move on the plan further
and we await the arrival of eternal despair
or immeasureable happiness
subsidiary - from temporal life.
Passing means to suffer the highest maturity
and that wisdom is an example for others,
that leads us to make our final moments
and that we can do more
if we only want to.

Maturing

We are mature when we finally understand
that when the time comes to leave family house
and when we know that finally
we have achieved something
and when we can hope now for ourselves
and we cannon rely on anybody.
Maturing is the period during which
we don't understand many things
and often, many things are anxious
and when we know that the responsibility
is coming to our shoulders
and when a young man is no longer a child.
We still don't understand many thing
in this life full of combats and suffering
but the time of maturation is preparing us for it
that when a young boy and girl is finally an adult
they can finally understand
that life is a game
in which you are continually forced
to fight for your survival
and not fun and happiness without a gram of sorrow.
Teens tend to mature stormy and not always humbly
but at the end of all this bears fruit
and we know that we have this period behind us
when we hear
that the responsibilities are greater than our abilities.

Time

Time passes through years unstopped
no one knows at all the day and hour,
it varies continually
from day to day it changes continually
and chases us throughout life – time
and if you'd have milions of clocks
you're still unable to catch
the charm of the time called passing.
Time drives through life dizzily
still setting for us pile of tasks to be performed
and values to be passed to others.
And still, we are it's prisoners
and even in those moments when you want to forget
for a moment
time can still reach us unannounced
and again it quantifies our whole life.

Piktogram

He have appeared on the grass
unexpectedly culminated in flowers
on the green meadow is created
and from the top is all green.
He appeared unannounced
and nobody knows how to explain
the magic associated with it.
From where it came to this lush grass?
From whom it's a signal for us?
One thing is sure that
entirely he's green
and green as the color of hope is well known.
And yet we know one thing,
that it's uncertain to think
because whatever we'll discover
it still remains on green grass
it's a sign of something
and not the phenomenon of the nature.

MacBeth

She used to sit on the bench always unforgettable
and she always had one thought -
to sown the fortunate throughout the world
she have been thinking a lot
but nothing specific could come to her mind
so she began the life with ideas
that were as eternal as faith in our hearts
and like child's love to his own mother.
When she paced the unknown lands
and provided people with signs of piece
she has reached the point at which she became aware
that beyond love people are not aware of faith.
So she still traveled
and she met various scholars
and on the way she healed people.
And unexpectedly she have come to the point in her life
when she became fully convinced of her achievements,
and she had planned sudden return on her way
through this hectic life
and heart full of blowing charm.

Faith

We believe and we believe
in the truths of life and eternal faith
and always convinced we pray for something
what is not always clear to us
but we know that we believe
and that the taste of belief is eternal in us
and that it doesn't matter what will come
and what we recently went through
so we continue to believe that it must be better,
that we'll receive grace and absolution
and everlasting joy
and care over our children will be given to us
despite all the wrongs and errors,
which we still commit in our life
But believing means to entrust
and confide our life to someone.

Dreams

They are coming to us in the night unexpectedly
always shocking and intriguing
dreams that create images in our head.
They amaze us with the colour of their transfers
and they are more interesting
when they're appearing longer.
They show our future
and portend forthcoming events
Like angels – they warn us this way,
the way in which we go through life,
in happiness and agitation.
We fall asleep, then dream and wake up
and so from day to day we do it cyclically.
Colored paintings surround our head
and sometimes it transforms into dark creatures
the most important is not to give them the faith
because they are only colorful pictures
and not determinants of survival or death.

Posterity

They lived once on this earth
Our dear sons
and even though they often sin
we are still drawing values from it.
We are learning from their ancient wisdom
how to live this life – relying on their advice.
And still we tend to wander
but they always watch and help us.
There is always a note of truth in primeval history
that we should learn the art of life from our mother
and other uncles deriving from her
because they were more resourceful in their days
than no one man that hails from the city
in the time of struggle.
And the tradition is always cultivated
because as say:
from grandfather to grandfather
are coming only noble truths
that imitating someone has never misleaded anybody
but thanks to it
people could gain more than they expected earlier.

Bleeding heart

Immense pain visits him in the chest
and it's impossible to describe his passion
the pain exceeds any known power
and indicates something which no-one
was able to understand.
He lays down,
because he can not withstand the pain
and still doesn't know
that it's his punishment
and not the result of unforeseen desease.
Tears are overflowing your heart
and you need to know one
that suffering is in human nature
and remembers every minute
 and stores them in itself
and when it gives to know about itself
it painfully turns us back
from the wrong way
And his despair is so expressive
like a bird flying in blue sky
he yelps strongly to recall himself to us
to return from this road,
which only leads us toward passion and death.

Happiness and desease

More than any pain
I can see a smile on your face
and I believe that one day you'll forget
but indeed you cannot
does unawareness is a salvation for us
or maybe the view of beloved child?
Illness is coming
and all forces are leaving us
but happiness in adversity is
that in close family and friends
you can see your own joy.
And most importantly
to make your own dreams come true
and not overly break down
and benefit from life as much as possible.
After these moments, however, comes the moment
in which we know
that we can not draw it any longer
and despite the constraints we feel fate
as we would jiggle among clouds
and as we could decide entirely about our fate
and our concerns are no longer important
because fortunate came to us
despite our internat depression.

To live better

To live better
you must always look after your own interests
assist another in need
so when we need help
others can give it to us.
It's always wise to remember
to donate own time to others
and not too seek to much to become rich,
rather lead humble life
and to be devoted our family.
The most important, to collect own money
and not lose them for stupidities,
rather for valuable matters.
Not being debauched and envious
can help as well
and above all
we shall trust others
that other may be in the need of spirit.
And most importantly,
we should focus our attention in God
and with all wories call for help
to him – always
like we're asking our good father
for the lessons on good manners.

Matthew

Young boy strolled on the green meadows
and he had so much bitterness withing his heart
that he forgot about his continued walk around the world.
He galloped through green lush
and encountered various personages on his way
Once he encountered a princess
strolling on the fields -
she sought flowers to the castle
in these green meadows.
Next was witch she was hungry for experiments
so she sought a frog jumping between meadows
but she has not found it and returned to her cottage.
Then time came for witch-doctor -
ha has looked for people willing to undergo his
treatment; he has been strolling around the world from
years but no one has acquired yet.
Then he met an old man
which have been walking as well
and he said to Matthew – my dear boy
and immediately the conversation started between both
and eventually it turned out to a point
in which Matthew found out
that old man lost his horse
he sought him in nearby forest
but could not find him.
And so the young boy chose
to go for a walk to find a horse
which walked in the forest not making a single noise.

Casablanca

Water beams there
and people eat ice creams in glasses
birds are singing there on the sky
and ships are arriving all the time
to welcome her beauty of hospitality
Beaming Casablanca
wakes up every morning
and falls asleep together with the herd of people
stalling through streets until pale morning.
She greets with it's charm newcomers
and is a purpose of dreams of many people
and for other residential place.
Here, many love stories happened
and many will still come
and most important
that her beauty will never quench
but is growing throughout years
and welcomes the crowds of those
who are in love.

The time of hope will come

Daily contemplation comes to him daily
and there are so many desires
that he still does not know
which are important and in need,
and which are an ordinary fabrications of nature
so he continually believes
that in this hope
that still remains in him
is a little bit of space for more
than just the needs of ordinary human existence.
Trying so much through hard work
and by the same time working with own hands -
and its his main merit -
he believes that after hard life
he'll receive deserved reward.
But he still doesn't know
that in order to get the reward
he has to be at pains for a bit longer
and then receive payment
for the labours of human faith.
Even though, he's full of hope
one day he'll come to a point
in which his desires will fulfill.

Traveler

He has been traveling around the world
and saw so many things going around
whatever somebody said
he noted it randomly.
He recorded the faces
and loved his mysterious adventures
and every time he returned home – he felt disgust
and traveled back.
Even though, the world not once was the enemy to him
and as many deseases as he had
and encountered many nasty behaviors
he still came back to these unknown pastures.
He still extended his trips
through continents and unknown fames
and more he saw and heard
it draged him more firmly and he saw
that his dream is to be in exile
and he wants to continue his trips boundlessly
and once he'll become an old man
he will settle for good
in the land of unknown adventure.

Lovers

The float in the air full of love
first they wisper and then they meet together again
and although presence is more important for them
than forthcoming future
they see their future in the clouds
like a dreams of a skylark
and they don't intend to release themselves
from this feeling
in which they are stuck up to their ears
covered, in the ties of love – focused in their eyes.
More they meet together
whirl more firmly snatches them
and they experience the love – unknown up till now
as young men they run through forests and meadows
and they hang flowers on each other's neck
and done with spring branches earrings.
And the symbol of love are their firm embraces
and an amazing experience,
which is running around the lake
full of the brightness of the moon
and other stars in the sky.
All of this is happening in the incredible enjoyment
but whether this love is so strong
to form a marriage followed by the responsibility
to keep their promises to the end of their life?
But one thing is certain, that their passion will be
eternal; the more they look at each other
the more they discover in themselves
and are connecting again.

Mystery

She is concealed in uknown place
and despite everything she will not be revealed
until she will be concealed by the relevant people.
And its content is still unknown to us
and even if the mountins could speak
they would not provide us with the content
concealed over the years.
In this mystery thoughts and expressions are enclosed
once transferred on the paper
and now kept in the brain rolls
and speaks to us so eloquently,
that the more we want to know it
the more difficult it is for us to learn something
and even worse to discover its origins
and intentional plans conceived in it.
But one day, someone will tell
and from legend it will come to the daily reality
and will tell about itself to not one concerned,
travelers and children with owl's memory

Through the forest

Through the forest we ran together
in the grip of faithful love
and by those greens we ran faithfully
and we believed
that one day our hearts will be together in the heaven
we walked so and still believed
that even thought there is a small spark of our dreams
our burning hearts will meet them
like a sorceress with a magic wand – full of fullfilment
Over those windy grasses and bushes
and all the night creatures
and wild animals living in it
we ran through this forest for better future for us
and we knew that one day we'll come to glade
where our house will rise
and uprising nest of love and dreams.
And even though the time still passed
and the seasons of the year were swinging -
we ran through the forest gasping for breath
and by the same time we were praying for better
tomorrow
and for this our greatest strength went with us -
a faith that guided us
for tomorrow's beauty... throught the forest...

I'll say

I'll say that I respect you
and as always I appreciate these things
that you do for me in spite of the will
and how everything
you're always aiming to me with respect as well
I'll say that I experienced a lot in my life
and the more experience I have
I especially appreciate
painful but at the same time helpful - life experiences.
I can say to you so many things
that I often experienced love in my life
that I cought the respect and friendship as well
and that despite everything I am still happy
and I do not want to change,
despite the general criticism
and I still want to grow up in this weird world
and continually experience things
which are strange and at the same time
they extend and develop into various dreams.
I'll say that I still want to grow up
and I do not want to ever stop
continually want to experience something
at the same time be with others
in the good and bad moments.
I'll say that life is such
what we can imagine
and I'll say that I fulfilled myself
and whether they are others fulfilled as well?

I am thinking about you

I think about you day and night
the more I'm focusing
the more I'm lost
in my mind I wander because I'm focusing on you
I'm continually walking from wall to wall
and I am still binding my joys with you
and even if I would undergone many roads
and saw many wonders of the world in galore
always in concentration
I'll stop and think
that you are somewhere in there, and I think
that my hope is you
and therefore I continually think about...
you joys and sorrows are mine as well
and I see my reflection by your side
the more I'm swinging in the clouds of dreams
the more I'm concentrating
and see my fiture at your side.

I thought once

I thought once
that I will fulfill myself in life
that my dreams will ever come,
that I'll reach heaven and even stars
that I'll meet new people
and rediscover the world
and that I'll pace many countries
I'll get to know customs, people
and will have a blanket full of adventures
and then I'll say to myself
that I did so many things
that I can be proud of it
and proudly praise all over
it will come to me once I'll grow up.
Because in the plans is such power,
that when you think everything is real
and still real until you'll wake up.
So every time I think so
and I'll think as long as I only can.

Ambitions

He had the ambitions
to conquer the world one day
to tramp all aspects of forest
to bring aid to children in African bushland.
He thought a lot, that he has to achieve a lot in his life
and he tried so hard
that he lost the sense of elapsing time
and one day he noticed something
that the lack of ambition is universal evil
but too big one often leads toward one -
lostness and discouragement
and therefore everyone must remember
to quantify their intentions so
they are in a position to carry them
and the rest will leave
until the time and effort will allow them to finish it
in the peace of soul
and conscience full of joy.

He went by the park

Once he went by the park
did not account time nor guards
he has passed subsequent benches
and surreptitiously dancing boys and girls
he shifted by green grass
and saw so much,
that in the end he settled up,
thought that he is already tired
So he decided to come back
and went on his way back
through these green meadows.
Once the crowd of happy people
have been breaking through
he realized
that his place is in this park
so he stayed there forever
he falled asleep and squat down
and stayed... forever...

Forgotten, he pallored...

He walked lonely
without apparent moment of joy
and when he tramped through his life
he noted that he has no family
and not too many friends as well.
His pallor frightened not one
he walked the streets
forgotten and abandoned
but no one wanted to help the homeless man
or even look for a wife for him.
We have no clue what happened
with this old, blinking man
it is unknown what is waiting for him
or even what he expects
from his life and crowd of dreams.

Children

They are born suddenly
and are growing up even faster
they ran through the world
and we are trying to keep up with them
but we need more forces
and our journey with them
is not such a lightweight.
Year after year they grow healthy,
they grow into a man and become pretty
and finally they fly away from our cottages.
At the end – they show us respect
and thank us that we helped them
and now they will try to do the same to us-
repay for all the conveniences in life
that they got from us
Our lovely children -
always faithful and dedicated to their parents.

All night passion

You are coming to me
in your passionate love
you look at me
and see my heart
All night passion is approaching
I'm thinking about you more often
and I want to experience
all the things you have in your mind
All night passion is rasing in me
and I still feel, what you are feeling
and we'll be together – forever
you'll stay – and we'll be together
We shall not let this moment escape
Let this night last all eternity
Let our love boom
Let our hands braid together
and let our hot bodies link together
let the all night passion fulfill
let it come in the end
you and I will connect together
and our love will fulfill...

Walking with her

I look up every morning
and see my belived one
she runs through the green forest
and she looks as if she's waiting for someone
is she waiting for me
or maybe for someone else
As she is strolling throught – she's looking around
asks about way the trees
and checks her beauty
in the reflections of lakes and rivers.
Passing through she encounters diverse nature
meeting new friends by the same time
she discovers herself
hitherto unknown
more I look at her
the more I want to come up
catch her body in my arms
embrace and kiss her
I want to run with her by the forest
and feel the fregnance of love
get to know the world with her
I want to experience magical moments
with her continually
and continue to move with her
through the moments of life.

I want to breathe

I want to breathe every day
enjoy the emerging sun
continue to look through the life
and plan my forthcoming future
exclude unknown lands
get to know new friends
and fully breathe my own life.
I want to breathe unknown things
and always want to keep in memory
unforgettable memories
I want to breathe intact freedom
I want to enjoy calm of my soul
and obsess fun places for me
and remember in their my joys
and even sorrows
and thanks to them continue to develop
and to be able to continue to breathe
the joy that flows from prose
of unknown to us life.

I saw once

I saw once her splendour
flashing in time
I tried chasing time
and follow her all the time
wherever its possible
and derive new informations
and still dream about unfulfilled
but written us acquaintance.
I would follow anywhere, anytime
and when I see you another time
I know that whenever I'll look
I'll follow her through
meadows, forests, rivers
and unknown lands as well
and I will overcome those barriers
and some day we'll know each other better
as the destination will link us together.
Finally, we will be happy
when we'll experience the taste of friendship
and we'll forget about botterness

I dreamed once

I dreamed once
for this time to come
so I can release myself with this moment
and begin to breathe all over
with the new reality
to overcome any barriers
and in my own thoughts fly away
and combine the forces again
and begin to live again
as it was never given to me
and thereby reappear
and feel the advent of changes
and feel that
I live again
and enjoy all I can.

New York

The splendour of neons
and continued taste of joy
diversity is great
and the unity among the people as nowhere else
perseverance and faith in the value is present here
and the assistance of neighbor is great
and respect for others immense
great, and as independent as nation
subject while open
New York is a dream of everybody
and everything is focused in it
and everything is about it
When you live here heart rejoices
because it expects that
new things will occur daily
and the stars in the media spotlight
swell even further in the eyes of their audience
even though streets are crowded
they always welcome us with their friendship
and you do not even know
that stranger can be the greatest friend
encountered accidentally.

Appropriately

Appropriately means reliably
with deference and focused attention
when you are asked for it.
You shall always behave appropriately
above all in the companionship
we must use appropriately our whole life.
The key is in proper nutrition,
cultivating sports
and live from day to day
not worrying about current issues.
Appropriately, that is to say duly
everything is provided in advance
and the seeds of excellence in this magic word lies.

I don't know

After that
as I entered in this world
and I met many people
and discovered many places
I do not know where I go
but I know that
I still aim somewhere
regardless of the weather
or from feeling
and the general desire of life .
I do not know where I'm going
nor what I want to achieve
because I'm still young
and I have the right not to know
and even more to deal with own reasoning
and continue to move for something
which is not always given to me.

Many ways

Following that
I go in this unknown world
and I'm still facing new
unjustified and still
undiscovered and ungovernable forever.
But I know that life
marks many roads
and we choose them
to then follow them - often in unknown
but mostly unforgettable
because even though memories are painful sometimes
they often heal and cure temporality
After all, we choose
and in fact we know
that with appropriate experience
ways are widen for us
and the experience comes to us
with the passing age.
Even though, there is so many ways to go
that sometimes I don't know
which one I shall follow
at least I know that I'm still following something
and this is better than standing in place
idle and shamelessly
when in the world there is so many ways to choose
from.

The splendour of love

It is known to us so
as own mother that knows the whole world
beams many hearts
passes with time sometimes
and regenerates back again
Splendour of love
I see him and sometimes I hear
I run to win it
and I'm always intimidated with its splendour
because with this brilliance
I want to follow toward the end of this world
and everyone is experiencing it at least once
in a life time
it does not depend from own luck
but pure, human reason.
So run now
for your own fortune
for your own brightness – for the love shine.

Effaced track

Even though, he was alone
and few he knew
he stalled often around the town
and sometimes he used to get lost in the crowd
or he tramped streets too excessively
sometimes he used to go into inappropriate places
and saw bizarre things
and had a whole range of experiences
and beyond that
is happened sometimes
that he used to take things
that didn't belong to him
and then he effaced tracks
to hide his deviations
so human crowd could see it
as everything is alright.

It happened, yes

Not once I had to walk hungry
and so lonely.
Thus, so that
I couldn't say good morning
because I didn't know anybody
and sometimes loneliness was so great,
that withdrawn
I crossed the streets
talking to myself, by the way.
But I always believed,
that everything will be fine
because earlier it used to be so
that not only loneliness troubled me
but I also cried from hunger and pain.
But now I know
that I can rely only on myself
because something that happened once
can continue to repeat in the future
and indeed, it might not happen once.

If you only want

In your blue eyes
so innocent and sweet
I look at them intently
I strain my sight to mature their beautiful charm
and I know subconsciously,
that I want to ask you
if you only want ...
and everything would be possible
so close now your beautiful eyes
and I'll also close mine
and we can think about our future, indeed
that all of those things could be so beautiful
and they all can become available to us
so open them again - your eyes
and I will cast a glance at you once
I'll imagine one thing for us
and then I'll leave
and you'll never see me again
with your beautiful eyes.

Your smell

It moves forward
the wind induces me
and in this reasoning I can feel a slight breath of smell
and yet, I don't know who is it.
I speculate and even conjecture
it's you – and now everything is like a sleep
and perhaps the fulfillment of dreams about you
Like summer flowers I can feel your smell
and I forget about the rest of concerns
and entirely on you I am focused.
I'm following you
in the hope of seeing you
and it appears that finally I cought you
but indeed, the smell has stopped for a moment
but right after it flew back.
And I'll continue to chase him
all over the place
to finally see you
I believe that I'll make it one day
I believe and I'll follow after this scent.

Fight

As samurai - it's time to fight
I continually have to face with unknown
and I'm fighting not even knowing
that money is not always the rate
but rather my haggard life – which is still rolling
I have to face with prejududices
as well as with human threats
Envy and longing are present
I take a backward glance, and again I'm fighting
about something that should always be mine.
Freedom and happiness
I'll be always fighing for it
I'll pass few more steps
I'll face with another banes
I will be a handful in the end
and I'll win to be at the forefront
because in life there is never too much of combat
for a better life.

Everything that...

Everything that I want today
be sure to remember it
I'll say it once
there and back in your arms
to heaven, to heaven
we will be together for longer time
in happiness and mourning
we'll go through this dark forest
and at the end happiness will meet us
and will stay between us.
Believe me, please
because I feel all so
to survive some more
and together enjoy happiness
and do not hesitate but tramp through life
as a missile hacking through
the clouds of heaven.

4th of July

Looking at the sky today
I see clear blue
as splitted freedom
I think once the second and third
and I can notice that
another independence day has come
toward the flag I'm addressing my love again
and swear loyalty and serving in need.
And even though I see evil around the globe
and not always everybody remember
to faithfully praise own country
so when I look at the calendar I see
that despite all everybody love our country
God bless America
everybody are calling
I subscribe to them
because freedom and happiness
you can experience here.

Through the streets of the city

Through city's streets
I'm walking until I'll get somewhere
just to be approached by someone
drunk or the happy one
walking around and singing.
No matter where I am
because I know everything here
this is my holy place
and here all of the names I know
through the streets of the city – I can see,
I see rich people coming from the city
and such others that are panhandling
and by the same time are wrapped in coats
and playing children as well.
and laborers working on construction
And going so all of those faces I meet
pleasure and confusion
richness and poverty I can see every morning.
Because the streets are full of human life
whenever I go
I face something new on my way.

My blue dreams

I go sleep once again
and even though I don't feel it – I'm falling asleep
and toward the next land I'm innocently aiming
and I see so many things
that I'm unable to repeat them
I'm recognizing things and many faces
but still I can not understand them well enough
so I fail to understand my own imagination
and I continually sink in it passionately
and whenever I'm getting out of it
I cry with child's tears
that good for me ended
and so, I'm beginning new trips
whenever I fall asleep
I don't know where I'll stop
and even that I can meet someone
and what all of this will mean for me
something good or maybe completely unknown.

Lap of luxury

It's unknown how
it's unknown from where
I see this gold hidden in the background
I want to touch it but I can't
at first I don't want but then I know
that the consequences for this will go.
Wealth is a great and wonderful thing
who live in it himself
has not yet appreciation
how much convenience is hidden in it
and even a lot of inspiration.
Richly decorated huts
all glitters a lot
and eyes are goggling at it even more precisely
Will it ever come to me
to live in such luxury
even if that could last only one moment
and maybe even all eternity.
This is all beautiful
glossy and unforgettable
when we see it
we always want more
and when we have it already,
usually we don't appreciate it.

Letters

He wrote once
how beautiful is the world
once he described
immense fortunate and temporary lack of happiness
so going by the world, noting
while living
he wrote to many people
but not too many responded
despite his sincere desire.
When he sends them
he always kissed the pages
and once they were already in the mailbox
he deeply regret that.
Letters were sent
but not always the responses were sent back
and this was creating a problem throughout
to faithful writer, poet
living on the edge of the streets in the city
whose name no one can identify
from the letters he sent
we don't know who he was
and what he was about in his life.

Colors

I look every day
admire but I can not hear
they have a different colour
but all are beautiful because they are true
the face has pink color
trees are green
moreover, such as fresh grass
because sometimes,
she has the color of a young hedgehog
Wheat sparkles with gold
and the sky is painted with blue color
Flowers are red
or maybe rare orange
and teeth are painted with opaque white
hair is black or brown
in the world we have only colors
I see them, and always admire
the more of them are
the more I'm amazed.

Let's dance

The time has come
and this is the appropriate time
we are stepping on the dance floor
to laugh and dance
and to have fun if we only senile forces
I put out my hands
you catch them
our pleached legs are sliding on the floor
and moving in this pace
we are whispering few words on power
we move in the right side
and we rebound back
to beat time with everybody because...
we're dancing
and we will dance forever
we hear cheers of joy
and I know that I will dance only with you
sometimes even slower,
but always and everywhere
I will be doing it with you
to be joyful and happy too.

Undiscovered time

It passes as glare
unknown to us time
yes, it's a time line
full of things to come
long, complex and full of classes
runs unstopped
and
through the next days
will show us how years are passing by
and how our youth evaporates
by the time when we'll realize that
we have more problems
and though
we are getting wise and serious
as the time goes by
and as we'll keep the pace with it
and keep the count of all the changes
at the end of everything
we will be able to square up from it.

In my own chair

I have sat in it not once
and I spread my hands as the brightness of sun
I put my legs on the table next to it
and I start to think
or rather contemplate
I am daydreaming or perhaps
I'm connecting with something in the reality
and it is beautiful,
that I have my place
on the right time
and I believe every day,
that it will wait for me as always
and will relax me as much as it can...
In my chair I sit and faithfully believe
that peace and quiet will accompany me
until this chair will be with me.
With black skin is made,
and makes sound when swinged
collapses under the weight of my body
after all, I know
that it's mine – always unforgettable
always relaxed me
and will relax me
until the end of each storm.

In my bed

I lie comfortably in my bed
and I look at your damp hands
I look on your face
I see your eyes and their immense brightness
I lie and think about something
that I can no longer lift the pain and suffering.
Many people visit me
everyone's talking – don't worry Jason
but I can feel in the depths of my soul
that there is a reason for my worries
and therefore, I can not sleep
and even listen to the birds singing in the morning
or joyous sounds of my grandson
One I know for sure
that it's comfortable for me right now – for sure
and only dream awakes in me hope
I am dreaming
and then things get back to the place.

Sailing through the world

I sail by myself
turning up my nose everywhere
I wave my hands to the other crews
to other countries
and people from different ships
We know that happiness is within us - and
always will be
wherever we are it will be there
everything is flying with us
memories, dreams, joys and sorrows
and even though we are far away
we remember
that we came from somewhere
and we have to go back there once
and everybody will wait for us with longing
and we'll greet us joyfully
running and crying in the arms of our children
But now we do not think about it excessively
we sail through life with our red boat
and no wave is a harm for us
because our love breaks them
before this wave gets us.

I saw the world

I have tramped so much – yes
I saw the brilliance of flowers
I have tramped so much – yes
I saw brightness of the golden stars
I have tramped so much – yes
I saw wild meadows
I have tramped so much – yes
I saw butterflies and wild bees
unknow wild carried me through the world
and unforgettable views
people that I wanted to know
cultures, which I wanted to discover
items that I wanted to touch
things that I wanted to try
pure curiosity led me so
led me so
throughout this wild world
At the end of this journey I realized
that I saw this world
I tramped it just like that.

The time of my career

I live so
and I have seen this world for a long time
I meet people from birth
and continually I learn something new
I graduated from school
and I already have wife
I run through life
always thoughtful
and finally I realized
unexpectedly at all
that I lead an adult's life
and I'm beginning my own career
and the new lifestyle
and I noticed unexpectedly
that I have more responsibilities
than time allows me to
but I'll roll up my sleeves
I will take all the businesses
and I'll solve them with the glace of coffee
until time allows me.

www.ingramcontent.com/pod-product-compliance
Lightning Source LLC
Chambersburg PA
CBHW031415040426
42444CB00005B/576